I ♥ Irn-Bru

Deedee Cuddihy

First Published 2012
Copyright © 2012 by Deedee Cuddihy

No part of this book may be reproduced,
except for short extracts for quotation or
review, without the written permission
of the publisher (unless it's the bits that
I borrowed myself, of course . . .).

ISBN 978-0-9551960-7-2

Published by Deedee Cuddihy
10 Otago Street,
Glasgow G12 8JH, Scotland

Cover design by R. Murray

Printed by (and design assistance
from) The Copy and Print Shop,
Gibson Street, Glasgow

Dedication

This little book is dedicated to all those people - friends, family, colleagues, acquaintances, total strangers - who shared their Irn Bru stories with me (and allowed me to take pictures) including Chris Scott, Fiona Davidson, Liz from Patna, Marion at the Philadelphia, "Jennifer" from Bridgeton, Lisa and, in particular, Stuart. And a special thanks to staff at the Apple Store in Glasgow for teaching me scary technological stuff - and Rosemary at Copy and Print for telling me I had to get to grips with it!

Everyone in my family drinks Irn Bru with their meals, except my gran. She only takes it with vodka.

(cafe assistant)

Paisley pensioner Jeanie Anderson (89) will be laid to rest today with a bottle of Irn Bru. Niece Molly Young said: "Jeanie loved Scotland's other national drink and requested that a bottle of Irn Bru should go in the coffin with her."

Irn Bru is the first thing I drink when I get up in the morning and the last thing I drink at night. Sometimes I'll drink it in the middle of the night as well, if I wake up feeling thirsty.

(Jennifer, NHS worker)

When questioned about Irn Bru, 85 per cent of people said: "Do you know it's more popular in Scotland than Coke?"

There was a joke going around that when Scotland got independence, we'd build a wall at the border and cement broken Irn Bru bottles along the top of it.

(Beverly, musician)

"I think if my eight-year-
old self could see me at the
Royal Albert Hall winning
a prize for playing Dr.
Who, he'd need a stiff shot
of Irn Bru."

(Scottish actor David Tennant)

I was having breakfast in a cafe in Edinburgh one Sunday, back in the '80s, when I noticed the Proclaimers sitting at the next table, both of them eating a fry up, reading the Sunday Post and drinking Irn Bru.

(Billy Gould)

Scottish crime writer Ian Rankin drinks Irn Bru two or three times a week. As a child, he mixed it with vanilla ice cream in the summer and says it is the perfect accompaniment to fish and chips as well as an excellent "restorative" after a boozy night.

Billy Connelly used to tell a story about a drunk man with a bottle of Irn Bru in one pocket of his jacket and a bottle of whisky in the other. The joke was that when the Irn Bru fell out of his pocket, the bottle was so strong it didn't break but when he bent down to pick it up, the bottle of whisky fell out – and broke.

(Tom Foy, Cowdenbeath)

Scottish craftsman John Creed has created a stunning sterling silver jug and tumbler set for Irn Bru drinkers. The jug's airtight stopper ensures the Irn Bru stays bubbly and the tumbler's gold interior reflects the drink's bright orange colour to infinity.

As a child, actor Sanjeev Kohli would make Irn Bru ice cubes to suck while watching Wimbledon.

"Thank goodness the problem has been Irn-ed out!" Scotland's First Minister, Alex Salmond on hearing that Irn Bru would not have to lose its famous Sunset Yellow colour.

"Despite the beaches, sunshine, culture and amazing food in Los Angeles, the lack of Irn Bru was a problem." Biffy Clyro manager Neil Anderson reveals that making an album in LA can be difficult for a Scottish band.

My wee brother got Irn Bru in his feeding bottle from when he was about nine months old. But you waited a minute before putting the top on or else it would be too gassy for him.

(Stuart, Cowcaddens)

It's not Christmas in Scotland until the Irn Bru adverts come on the telly.

The guys in my office get really excited when a new Irn Bru ad comes out. First they watch it over and over again on You Tube. Then they reminisce about all the old Irn Bru ads.

(Iain, graphic designer)

I'm not like the typical type of older Chinese person who lives in Scotland. I don't smoke, I don't gamble - and I drink Irn Bru.

The taste of Irn Bru is just
like a traditional
children's drink, made
from pears, that we have
in North East China,
where we come from.

(Chinese girls studying in Scotland)

I've got a pal who has Crohn's disease but instead of taking a lot of drugs, he prefers to keep it under control with a small amount of vodka in a big glass of Irn Bru.

(Mark, call centre worker)

My friend is so addicted to
Irn Bru, we joke that her
ginger coloured hair
would turn white if she
ever stopped drinking it.

(Marie, office cleaner)

I accidentally dyed my hair a weird orangey colour and when I told people I'd used Irn Bru, they believed me.

(Shan, artist)

Ian Wright, 46, from Plean
in Stirlingshire is so
addicted to Scotland's
other national drink, he
spent £175 getting an Irn
Bru can tattooed on his
leg.

I love Irn Bru but I'd never have it in my whisky.

(Jim, postman)

Our local Lidl in Spain
sells all the essentials:
marmalade, oven chips -
and Irn Bru.

(Maggie)

Irn Bru is always available here at the Gleneagles Hotel. It's part of Scottish culture. Americans like to try it, many of our guests have it with vodka and it's something the kids can drink.

We have Irn Bru on sale in our Food Market all the time; in glass bottles and cans. (Harvey Nichols department store, Edinburgh)

When I opened my cafe, I said I was only going to stock fruit juices and smoothies but I finally had to get in some Irn Bru because so many people asked for it.

(owner, Alba Cafe)

Why do I have Irn Bru on sale in a health food shop? I asked the person I bought the business from the same question. It's because there's a bus stop outside and drivers come in and ask for it. Occasionally they also buy a bag of organic crisps – and even some vitamins.

An American came in and said he'd been told he had to try Irn Bru. I said: "Are you sure?" He must have liked it because he was back four days in a row for another can.

(shop keeper)

All the 'workies' drink Irn Bru on our building site. Bottles are best, then cans. Plastic's not so good because it goes flat quicker.

(Tommy Cunningham, plumber)

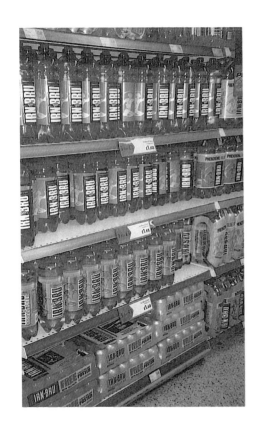

We had builders in doing
some work on our house
and the first thing they
did when they arrived in
the morning was put their
bottles of Irn Bru in the
fridge.

(Maureen)

We lived next door to my gran and she always used to have her friend in at the weekend for a drink. She'd have a quarter bottle of whisky with Irn Bru and her friend would have Bacardi and Coke.

(Sara Duff, Paisley)

Irn Bru is the best cure
for a hangover.

(At least 100 people)

If I want Irn Bru on a Sunday, I've got to get to my local shop early or they've sold it all to people with hangovers. And that's in Edinburgh!

(Pete, ex-army)

In Kilmarnock, a common cure for a hangover is a can of Irn Bru and a Mars Bar.

(John, museum assistant)

I drink half a bottle of Irn Bru first thing in the morning for my hangover. That's all you need to deal with the head, the stomach and the thirst. Once you've burped, you feel fine again.

(Bill)

I took Irn Bru all the time
for my hangovers - until I
stopped drinking. I'm a
recovering alcoholic now.

(Margaret)

My brother used to put a bottle of
Irn Bru on the windowsill in our
bedroom at night if he'd had too
much to drink but needed to get up
for work the next day. I slept in the
bottom bunk and, in the morning,
I'd pass the Irn Bru up to him, he'd
take a few swallows and that would
be his hangover sorted. He was 19
and I was 18.

(Martin)

Irn Bru for a hangover?
No. It's water for a
hangover and Irn Bru if
you want a sugar rush.

(gallery owner)

Irn Bru's a minority drink in England. So when I moved to Scotland, it was incredible to see, not just the amount of Irn Bru on sale everywhere, but actual Irn Bru fridges.

(Nick, recruitment executive)

A friend visiting from down south said he was surprised to see Irn Bru on sale here. He thought it was something they only drank in his home town - Manchester.

(Karen, librarian)

My brother-in-law says the Irn Bru he gets in Sheffield doesn't taste as good as the Irn Bru in Scotland.

(Hare Krishna guy)

Irn Bru fudge from the Ochil Fudge Pantry - I'm definitely an addict now!

(blog post)

Irn Bru "reduction" for ice cream, sorbet, fudge, tablet, cakes, icing etc. :

Pour 330 mls of Irn Bru into a pan and bring to the boil. Simmer until it has reduced to around 100 mls. This will take about 20 minutes. Cool before use.

My favourite treat as a child was a scoop of Italian-style ice cream mixed into a glass of Irn Bru; not as a 'float' but a drink.

(Mae, office worker)

If I want something sweet,
I love a glass of ice cold
Irn Bru with a scoop of
Mackie's vanilla ice cream
in it.

(Barbara, singer)

I used to go with my gran to a cafe in Barrhead and have a glass of Irn Bru with ice cream in it. I loved it.

(Amanda)

If you were an insulation engineer in the shipyards in Govan, you used to get free Irn Bru because you were working in boiling heat in a confined space. You could only do half an hour before you'd have to come out and drink a whole bottle of Irn Bru. I probably got through eight bottles a day during a shift.

"Here, get this down your thrapple. A swally of Irn Bru. Cheers big ears."

(from "Three Nights and a Sunday", a play about the Clyde ship yards, written for schools by Brian Whittingham, commissioned by Glasgow Museums' education department)

"It was tough hearing I would need to give up Irn Bru." A 32-year-old Aberdeen man on being diagnosed with Type 2 diabetes.

IRN BRU IN BOLIVIA!!! It was on the menu at a curry restaurant in La Paz. We ordered two cans but were devastated to learn they were sold out.

(blog post)

Went downstairs earlier and just about started crying 'cause there was no Irn Bru! Then I found out my mum had put it in the cupboard.

(Twitter)

I had mega cravings for Irn Bru when I was pregnant with both my kids. The vending machine at work never did so much business!

(internet forum)

We ran out of Irn Bru last night. I CAN'T SURVIVE WITHOUT IRN BRU!

(Twitter)

We found Irn Bru in a supermarket near Mt. Kilimanjaro. Alas, it was warm so we buried it in the frozen vegetables cabinet to cool down while we did a tour of the store.

(blog post)

Tidying my room and
found 24 empty Irn Bru
cans. Oops.

(Twitter)

Alison and John had a retro Scottish wedding reception at the St. Vincent Street Bowling Club in Glasgow with kilts, dancing, Tunnocks Tea Cakes - and Irn Bru!

(blog post)

There must have been a time when there wasn't Irn Bru - but I can't remember it.

We do an annual tour for the public around our Irn Bru factory here in Cumbernauld. Last year, 300 people signed up for it before we had to open a waiting list.

The only juice ma weans'll drink is Irn Bru.

(man in the street)

The thing my daughters look forward to the most on their birthdays is Irn Bru. It's the only time they're allowed fizzy drinks.

(Garth, managing director)

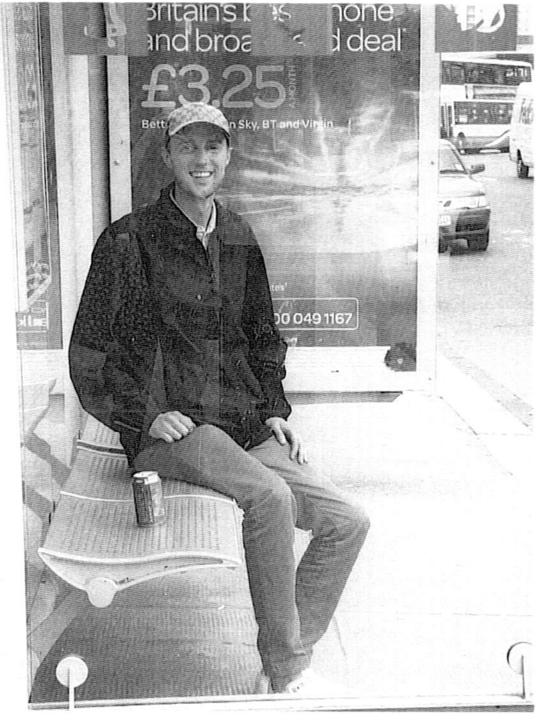
£3.25

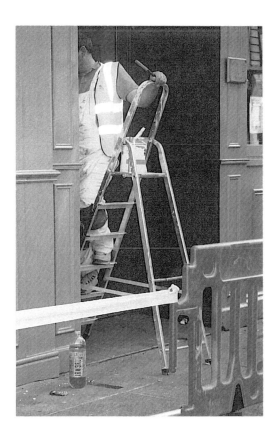

My friend Lesley has a horse called Sam who likes Irn Bru. Sam holds the glass bottle between his teeth and Lesley tips it up so he can drink it.

(Rosemary, printer)

Our budgie loves Irn Bru
and if you try to stop him
drinking it out of your
glass, he bites you.

(Charlene, Kirkintilloch)

I don't think my dog's addicted to Irn Bru but if he sees me drinking it, he puts his tongue out and I pour some into his bowl.

(Pat, care worker)

When questioned about Irn Bru, 99 per cent of Americans said: "It tastes exactly like Bazooka Bubble Gum."

"I'm very thirsty. I'm thirsty too. Here's the drink that's made for you - Barr's Irn Bru!"

(Barr's jingle)

My preferred fizzy drink is Irn Bru and my preferred alcoholic drink is vodka - but I never mix the two together. When I'm having a vodka, I put Coke in it.

(Jeanette, Cumbernauld)

I've drunk Irn Bru all my life. I must have been bottle-fed it as a baby!

(Val, post office assistant)

My flat mate can get through a two litre bottle of Irn Bru when he's watching the telly. It's not a pretty sight.

(Jonathan, medical student)

We get through about 12 cans of Irn Bru a day in my family so it's quite an expensive habit.

(Clair, mum and office manager)

Scottish Asians are big Irn Bru drinkers. My family gets through 12 bottles a week but I've got a butcher working for me in the shop who is in the Premier League of Irn Bru drinkers: 18 bottles a week.

(business owner)

I buy 12 bottles of Irn Bru every Friday and that usually does me for the week.

(Stevie)

My first year at uni down in England, I celebrated Burns Night on my own with an M&S single portion haggis cottage pie and a can of Irn Bru.

(Kate, teacher)

I never eat anything
before 11 in the morning
but I'll buy a can of Irn
Bru and drink that on my
way to work.

(Mikey Snee)

I take a glass of cold diet Irn Bru up to bed with me every night. Sometimes I drink all of it before I go to sleep; sometimes I leave a little to have if I wake up feeling thirsty.

(Fiona, lawyer)

A familiar sight in Glasgow in the 1980s used to be neds in shell suits, with a big bottle of Irn Bru sticking out of one of the trouser pockets.

(Lisa, personal trainer)

My gran didn't think it
was safe to drink tap
water unless you boiled it
first so the family drank
Irn Bru instead.

When my mum was a girl
in Ayr, they used to get
Irn Bru delivered to the
door every week by
someone they called The
Ginger Man.

(Laura, student)

Our gran called the person who delivered her Irn Bru The Juice Man. It came in glass bottles in a crate.

(Sherly and Aimi from Clackmannanshire)

The Ginger Man would come to the house on a Saturday afternoon to collect the empty Irn Bru bottles and leave a crate of new ones.

I used to work at the Barr's factory
in Glasgow, loading and unloading
the lorries for the guys who sold Irn
Bru around the doors. Sometimes I
was slipped a free crate to take
home with me.

School pupils in Aberdeenshire have created a new dish for a local restaurant, featuring onions sauteed in Irn Bru.

"I used a mixture of Irn Bru and breadcrumbs - and the fish loved it! They were jumping on to the hook."

Angler Crawford Griffiths from Castle Douglas making big claims for his new bait recipe.

I like the taste of Irn Bru
but I hate the colour so I
only ever drink it from a
can.

(Val, graphic designer)

In primary school, the teacher was reading out our Healthy Eating diaries and one of my friends had written down that she had a can of Irn Bru and two packets of pickled onion Monster Munch for breakfast – every day.

(Rosie O'Murray, director, Creative Solutions)

"I was surprised that my team mates ate crisps and drank Irn Bru – even in the bus on the way to matches."

Former Celtic player, Shunsuke Nakamura on the differences between top athletes in Scotland and Japan.

"Underdogs Brechin City have a secret weapon to try to upset Rangers today – Irn Bru. Players guzzle down gallons of the fizzy drink – and hope it will give them the edge as they face Ally McCoist's newco side in their first ever match."
(The Sun, July 29, 2012)

No one in my family drinks tea or coffee. It's always Irn Bru.

I'm not an Irn Bru addict
but I can't go for long
without getting a wee
notion for it.

(catering worker)

My parents don't understand the emotional connection I have with Irn Bru. That's because they weren't born in Scotland and I was.

(Kevin, musician)

"It's the duty of every Scot to support our home product - Irn Bru."

Kenny MacAskill, SNP MSP

If you're Scottish, you feel it's your patriotic duty to drink Irn Bru.

In Scotland, we love Irn Bru because it's made by Scots, for Scots.

I drink Irn Bru to keep
Coke knocked off the
number one perch.

(Doug, bar worker)

I always take a bottle of
Irn Bru with me on a bus
journey.

(Liz, Patna)

Jack Daniels - meet Irn Bru. You two are going to be very happy together.

(blog post)

When I first arrived in Glasgow from Saudi Arabia, I wondered: what is this orange liquid that everyone is drinking? Then I found out - it was Irn Bru!

(PhD student)

I always insist my friends from abroad try Irn Bru at least once when they come to stay with me.

(Mary, therapist)

The only gift my German god daughter asks me to bring her when I go over for a visit is a can of Irn Bru.

(Kristin, doctor)

I have to bring my niece
Irn Bru when I go back to
see my family in Holland.
She got a taste for it when
she was visiting me and
you can't get it over there.

(Hans)

My partner is Hungarian and when her nieces and nephews came over for a visit, we laid on Scottish stuff like haggis, square sausage and Irn Bru. And they really took to the Irn Bru – which surprised me. I can see me having to make room in my case for some when we go to see them.

(library assistant)

Irn Bru isn't something I normally have in the house but whenever my two nephews are visiting from England, they make me buy it for them.

(Cath, deli manager)

I've seen Irn Bru on sale in Egypt and the Canary Islands.

My friend's son moved to America and when he comes back home for a visit, he always requests the same first night dinner: a fillet steak and a can of Irn Bru.

(Malcolm)

I'm not an Irn Bru addict but I like to know it's available. That's why I get so excited when we're abroad and I see it on sale in a shop. My husband always says: "Calm down, Mary – it's only Irn Bru."

To my horror, I discovered that Irn Bru was difficult to get in Wales when I went to uni there. Fortunately, a local shop keeper agreed to order a supply in just for me.

(Adam, film maker)

I was in a hotel in Nottingham for a wedding and when I asked for a vodka and Irn Bru, the barman said: "You're in England now, love; we don't have Irn Bru."

(Lorraine, Bridgeton)

People say you can't get
Irn Bru in England but I
was in Watford recently
and saw an Irn Bru lorry
near the train station.

(Terri, journalist)

We went on a family holiday to Florida about 12 years ago and my niece, who was 10 at the time, just couldn't understand that there was a place in the world where you couldn't get Irn Bru.

(Craig McLeod)

When my friend's daughter was in America working in one of those summer camps, she kept texting her mum saying how much she was missing Irn Bru. They threw an Irn Bru surprise party for her when she got back.

(Chris)

I've got friends who, when
they fly back to Scotland
from a holiday abroad,
head straight to the
airport shop to buy some
Irn Bru as soon as they
get off the plane.

(Darren, pub manager)

We sell a lot of Irn Bru in our International Arrivals shop.

(WH Smith, Glasgow Airport)

When I saw Irn Bru on
sale in Ibiza last summer,
I felt so proud.

(Pete, charity worker)

My mum used to pretend she'd kicked her addiction to Irn Bru but she was hiding the bottles in the mop bucket.

(Marion, chip shop)

I'm missing my girlfriend,
my dog and my Irn Bru.

(Scottish soldier in Afghanistan)

Deedee,

A colleague passed on your question regarding Iron Bru (sic). I am afraid we do not sell Iron Bru in any House of Lords refreshment facilities.

Regards,
Owen Williams,
Head of Press and Media,
House of Lords.

Dear Deedee,

Thank you for your recent email. I have contacted a colleague within the House of Commons Banqueting Department who has informed me that Irn Bru is not sold within the House of Commons. I hope this is helpful.

Yours sincerely,
Debbie Cesvette,
Information Office,
House of Commons

Hello Deedee,

Irn Bru, along with a variety of other soft drinks, is made available to MSPs to buy at the canteen in the garden lobby which is managed by our external caterers. I hope this is helpful.

Thanks,
Kirsty Rimmer,
Media Relations Officer,
Scottish Parliament

About Deedee Cuddihy

Deedee Cuddihy is a journalist who was born and brought up in New York but has lived in Glasgow since the "Big Storm" of 1967 (which she slept through). Or was it 1968? After finishing art school in Glasgow, she realised being an artist would be too difficult - and being an art teacher would be even more difficult. So she became a journalist and has been one ever since. She is married to a Scotsman and has two grown up children - plus two granddaughters. "I Heart Irn Bru" is the sixth in her popular Scottish Mini Books series, the other titles being "Under the Skin of the Scottish Tattoo", "The Little Book of Scottish Men", the best-selling "How to Murder a Haggis", "Would Jesus Wear a Kilt?" and "Scottish Wedding Disasters." She drinks Coke.